BEAUTY IN THE LET GO
DIRTY SWEET POETRY
TIFFANY SIMONE

Beauty In The Let Go
Copyright © 2018 - 2020
by Tiffany Simone

2nd Edition

"She is evidence that there is magic in this world... that ONE. She came around to show you life through new eyes, that wonders never cease, and you are ready for new things."

And this poem from Tiffany's first volume of poetry *Butterflies & Skin* describes her writing to absolute perfection. She does not disappoint in her second poetic offering Beauty in the Let Go either. In this book she continues to highlight her all-encompassing talent that has led to an amazing social media following. She knows that within every heart lies a romantic core, and that it is longing to be stroked in just the right way.

Tiffany is a fireball of timeless and reserved heat. A Chicago native, she resides there with the two bright stars of her world, her children. A romantic adventurer at heart, she is a compilation of a heartache survivor and butterflies at sunset. While others write in metaphorical styles, she chooses instead to offer life experiences in carving her verses. Her words are absorbed in such an authentic and gut punching way that the reader will carry the words in their souls long after the last page.

If you are a fan of her first book *Butterflies & Skin*, then you will love the transition of how *Beauty in the Let Go* delves deeper into your internal layers. Pour a glass a wine, unbox the chocolates... and unwind.

Tiffany writes for release, and she wants you to feel it too.

-Alfa
Bestselling Author of Abandoned Breaths and I Find You in the Darkness

To Hope

Thank you for staying with me.

Butterflies are deep and powerful representations of life. Around the world, people view the butterfly as representing endurance, change, hope, and life.

INTRODUCTION

I remember getting my first butterfly tattoo and thinking…
I should feel this pain because I'm wrong.
Technically still a child, yet already I'd been made to feel broken,
someone not worthy of love.
A tattoo inked onto young troubled skin will feel like Heaven. It will feel
like a giant sigh of relief
because it's identifiable pain, something physical, instead the mass
confusion inside your head.

Over time I broke.
  I healed.
  I really really broke.
  I asked for help.
And when I chose to, I fixed myself.

Today, I continue to live in a constant state of self awareness. I listen
to my brain, my body, and my fears. I try my best to stay away from
toxicity and triggers.
I blurt out my honesty with what I feel is an unattractive vulnerability.
But it's me. And now I make the rules.
The past is not irreversible. "Damage" will not define me. Not all of our
stories are full of memories that want to be retold for the sake of
laughter and smiles.
And truthfully, what's behind me has better prepared me for what life
has given me now.
I am a better mother. I am a stronger woman. I have more appreciation
for life, loving harder and with fierce loyalty. And I'm damn proud of
myself.

Hey past bullshit, you lose, I win.
I fucking win.

I've gotten several little butterfly tattoos since that first one.
However, unlike that time each one represents a moment
wonderful to me.

Become a work in progress.
Make yourself a work of art.

The darkness can be tantalizing. It can draw you in with its smooth-edged comfort.
I don't want to stay there though. We don't grow in the dark. Becoming more means walking forward, looking up and seeking knowledge consistently.

Your past has shaped you. Put it to the side. Let's see this warrior version too.

It's amazing...there truly is BEAUTY IN THE LET GO.

If it is love you need, I will love you here on these pages.

Welcome to my imagination, play with my words.

Writing to heal,
Tiffany Simone

ENTRANCE

I have a way of making an entrance…
and I can promise you it will always include being late,
everyone staring,
and hoping I look cute enough to be forgiven.

(She's an old school romantic with a sassy bad girl side.)

INVITE ME

Invite me in.
Show me all the places you've been neglected and
slowly undress this reoccurring sadness.
I think our mouths might be full of answers tonight.

MY RULES

I said we should go slow...
but you still must remain completely occupied with
all things pertaining to me.

TO HOLD HER

Pulling her in, just a little bit rough by the small of her back...
she fits right in that spot against your chest.
Leaning to one side, she lifts herself, hands wrapped, burying
her face in your neck. Inhale. Sigh. This closeness makes the
two of you moan almost instinctively every time.
You know her eyes are closed and her mouth smiling.
You know she's already warm where her gorgeous legs meet,
and if you were to take this moment anywhere else, nothing
would stop the passion and heat.
You know she wants in, under your skin, like you want under
hers. Trust has given way and close is no longer enough.
Kissing her neck, you give her chills and hear her soft laugh
as she arches her smooth back.
Sweetly you kiss her eyes, while grabbing her ass harder.
She is a primal need, stopping is not an option.
And all you can think each time you fall into her like this is
...MINE.
and yes.
and yes.
and yes.

WARM-HEARTED

You are so oddly warm hearted in a world gone cold.
A life without passion would leave you freezing to death.
Hang on, there is fire ahead.

CRASH

When the emotions come, they all crash.
I apologize for the way you get swept up in the waves of
my dirty,
my sweet,
my everything.

(Don't let anyone else's definition of passion affect how loud
you need to yell.)

WATERY EYES

I have too much water that drips from my eyes,
that covers my face,
that runs off my jaw,
and slips through the sharp dips of my collarbone...
in some sort of crazy race to protect
my raw open heart.

(Water is cleansing. Tears give release. One day, let there be
no more apologies.)

GOOD THOUGHTS

Tell me anything.
Tell me something.
Give me good thoughts to dream about.
Say I'm more than pretty.
That's how you see me.
Maybe it's the way you know my mouth.
Just give me words
to keep like diamonds
when the silence is too much.
So tell me anything,
just tell me something…
true words I'll believe
without a doubt.

TIP TOE KISSES

I was made to hold hands,
to get close
and to be pulled up,
kissed on my tippy toes.

HEAR ME

I hope you see this vulnerability
for what it is.
Brave.

True.
Sexy, raw and revealing.
Hear me getting naked for you.

LIGHTNING HEART

One day I will strike correctly with my lightning heart,
and it will burn us through the thunder and the rain.
The only pain will be that which
you gently but passionately inflict on purpose,
as I pour my storms into you.

(When I give myself, I give you everything.)

STRAIT JACKET

There will be times
when she tries to hide her face
and wants to escape.
You've got to hold her tighter then.
Be her straightjacket,
because she is scared to crazy.
This is when she needs the loudest evidence
that you are a safe thing.

HUSH

I fell in love under a waterfall
 on a random summer weekend.
Letting the words stay in my head,
 my heart was too full, too heated.
Forcing some patience, my lips pouted a bit,
 but remained tightly sealed.
I'd worried about everything my vulnerable eyes
 might have revealed.
Giant shudder. Gentle sigh,
  ...a body absolutely needing to scream
 for fear of a mouth betrayal.
The number of times I'd repeated the words to myself
 didn't count.
I simply wasn't ready to let those precious I LOVE YOUs
 actually slip out.

INTENSITY

He craves me so intensely.
Even when I'm alone,
I'm surrounded
by his want.

HEART-SHAPED EYES

We slow danced just as I had dreamed of, big hands pulling
me closer and still closer on happy, twirling hips.
I felt a bit intoxicated. Your eyes, your smell, the music...
I was drunk on all of it.
You were standing oh so closely - focusing past the glassy
green and into my heart-shaped eyes.
I held onto you like you were my hero. I looked up at you like
you were my knight.
My feet were surely three inches off the floor.
There was a crowd, but I heard nothing but my feelings.
The clouds wouldn't let me down.
Within my chest there was a humming,
butterflies and hearts in a wrestling match.
Anything logical in me had clearly died.
I was in fairytale love that night.
You were standing oh so closely, staring once again, past the
glassy green and into my heart- shaped eyes.

BRAT

I'm a firecracker.
I'm a plot twist.
I'm a bad mood
and a thunderstorm,
but you'll like it.
In those fantasies my request is...
It's you and I
and I for you.
There's nothing for one another
we wouldn't do.
So put my name in your mouth
and make sure you like the way it sounds.
Because I want it all.
And I want it now.

(I will be your favorite...something you can not bear to take
your hands off of.)

UNCOMPLICATED

Sometimes it can get so complicated,
but the truth is it should be beautifully simple.
I don't know how he sees the things he does in me,
loving more
through the ups and the downs
and the rough and the soft of me.
To him,
this is simple.
I just love you. And love is love and you are love.
To him, I make perfect sense.

STOMACH

So, I wait.
I carry hope around like it is part of my own body,
and the butterflies dance in my heart.
They flutter and play,
waiting for their rightful day
to take flight into my stomach.

CHALLENGING

Prepare for me.
Get ready for this and all that I bring,
because I will not be something quiet sliding into
bed beside you.
Make sure to be the best, strongest and
most confident version of yourself when
you cross the threshold to my soul.
I promise I am much more than you bargained for.
I am ugly crying, panic attacks,
worried phone calls and shaky hands.
I am trying to scare you away.
Seven years of bad luck to the one who tries to stay.
I dare you to love somebody whose beautiful comes the
broken way.

(Are you still there?)

DELICIOUS

You tasted like sunshine and sangria.
You tasted like ocean salt and a bit like sin.
You were something whole,
something almost too much,
somewhere destined to begin.
You tasted like my own heart,
and definitely all my weight,
like I was the body you begged to belong in.
You tasted a bit like fate.

(To everyone else I was poison, but to him I was the only cure.)

HYPNOTIZE

I like the way your eyes follow me like they do.
This dress was put on with the sole purpose of hypnotizing you.

(I'm going to take my sweet time watching you, watching me,
all night.)

SOAKING WET

Wide awake and barely breathing-
I want to wear you like a storm.
Saturate me with love
and soak me in good intentions.

YOURS

There is no place I'd rather be than right here in the
way that you look at me. I want to be trapped in your
ocean-green eyes and live in your mouth.
Lick me with those pretty thoughts you have.
Wrap me in the naughty ones,
and then with your rough hand,
a little smack to the ass…
off to bed my good girl.

LIKE YOU DO

All my ends have split.
My edges dulled to nothing.
I believe I've come undone.
Please bring your bigger than mine hands
and gently hold my face.
Kiss me like you do when
you bring me back to safe.

YUM

I love the way that you talk to me. I
want to take each word you say
and eat it right out of your mouth.

WILD

With his hands on my hips, and my eyes on the sky,
I'm loud and I'm wild,
making love to the night.

SLAY

I stabbed him three times:
Once, for even looking at me.
Twice, because I became a believer,
and the third time, that was for making me weak.
I twisted it in further, making sure to hit bone.
That was for your cowardice.
I'm one hundred times better off being alone.

GUARD DOWN

I watch his back as he pulls me through the crowd.
Loving the grip of his big hand around my small one.
I smile inside and my guard falls.
The music blasts loud and the lights dance low.
He swings around to face me, his mouth finding mine.
It's the kiss that tells me everything I want to know.
My heart says I can follow.

DANGEROUS

It's in her eyes.
You can see the fear mixed with the happiness,
the open wounds begging to be covered by her brand new
attitude.
It's no secret though,
she'll always be a little bit dangerous.

(I think I'm starting to get a reputation for being a
heartbreaker; danger with a doll face.)

BASEMENT TAPES

She is the storm and the calm,
the right and the wrong...
nothing makes sense but she's like your favorite song.
And we only like the rain when it stops.

DEMONS

The demons will want to feast on your chaos.
Tell them to fuck off; there's love at your core.

LESSONS

Pretty plus pretty doesn't equal chemistry in much the same
way opposites won't always attract.
Life will hurt a million times before it starts to feel good,
and truly everyone will say they understand,
yet you'll always be misunderstood.

VERSION 2.0

I don't know this version of me.
I am one. I am both.
I am everything…
There are seven different passions fighting to emerge,
and all I want is a heart-beat type of home.

BOTH

She was like a fireworks show with all those beautiful colors.
To know her was to love her even when the sky went black.
Honestly, she could make the dark look damn sexy.

MORE THAN WORDS

I remember how we instantly held hands,
how ridiculously handsome your face was,
and how somehow without saying the actual words
you made me feel like the prettiest girl in the world.

CONTROL

Her goal is to embrace the moments,
play in their light,
but never ever let the emotions swallow her whole.
She wants control of the roller coaster.

WORRIER

Terrified to crazy,
a bit too much to handle…
all because I more than like
the way you smile
when you're staring at my face.

PHOTOGRAPH

Camera ready.
"Look at me," your mouth said.
I forced my eyes up.
Nothing is more vulnerable than showing you this love.
Camera down. You see it.
"I've fallen," says your eyes.
We pause in a state of staring;
A contest I will always lose to you.
The sky is looking beautiful ahead.
"Definitely," says your smile.

DIRECTIONS

The love we give is an explanation.
Pay attention please, because this is how I need to be loved.
This is what I crave.
I call you 'Handsome,'
because I want 'Beautiful' to be my name.
I tell you "I need you,"
because I wish you'd admit to needing me too.
The love we give is an explanation.
I'm showing you directions to me.

(This is important.)

KEEP

Loving it all
means hugging the
dark, holding the fear,
cuddling the sadness and kissing it clear.
I am a grey area with rainbows.
So wear your best,
but bring a change of clothes.
Ride with me and die for me.
Let me come apart in your hands.
Bring me back with three little words
that you don't throw around,
because once I fall in,
you must not let me down.

US

Us,
the ones with the cracks and scars…
we turn our pain into power.
We bring truth to the surface and dance in its honor. I
am not what broke me.
I am wild and beautiful and gloriously free.

DESTINED TO FAIL

The thing was...his voice didn't go soft when her eyes got quiet,
and it didn't get deep and growly when she pulled herself closer.
Maybe they didn't make sense because he couldn't love, and she
was love.
And if there was ever a tear, he turned away, closed off instead
of closer. Yet, she felt this irrational pull because she wanted
skin, and breath on her neck and hand
holding and hugs from behind,
and mine, and mine, and mine.
But he gave deadlines on those sorts of things. He feared the
future and would only talk about the present.
There was only so close his hands would go, and his mouth wasn't
hungry. It seemed to make a mockery of how much she wanted
and was willing to fall.
He sent music instead of words and she struggled to find clues
in things that weren't there, reprimanding herself for playing
detective with someone who admitted to only being a simple
man.
She never did feel safe. Already having had her fair share of
landslides and sinkholes, she craved solid ground,
when he wanted the wind.
She cried for the friendship that was lost.
This is what he had predicted would happen.
He had them set up to fail.
So they did. Another story of not meant to be.

(You were a punch in the stomach when I wasn't even looking for
a fight.)

FIREWORKS

If you don't like my fireworks, get the fuck out of my sky...
because I know I have a heart overflowing with love
and I look damn good tonight.

HYPERACTIVE BUTTERFLIES

You leave me with hyperactive butterflies in my stomach.
They want to fly up through my throat
because they ache for your lips as much as I do.
But I choke with laughter, and reprimand them.
Butterflies, his lips are mine.

TRUE OR FALSE

This is based on a true story that never happened.
These are actual facts covered in lies.
I am inspiration mixed with an overactive imagination.
Broken down, it's really just ink
  telling you
    healing me and
              passing time.

BOSS

You don't get to come back into my life
as if your name hasn't been trapped in my mouth,
and etched upon my heart for the past year.
No, I'm in charge of the rules now.

VULTURES

All the vultures swooped in mistaking her for fresh meat. She could only laugh at their lack of integrity and heart, while keeping her eyes focused on sincerity and a new start.

AFTER TASTE

When you're hungry with a craving,
    a desperate starving feeling...
    it's because of me.
Unfortunately
    that bitter aftertaste
        is your grieving.
Some poor choices were made
        when you decided
to clear your plate of someone
    as delicious
    as myself.

BLONDE HAIR BLACK MOOD

I can be mass confusion in a party dress.
  Pay no attention. No, wait. Please stay.
I am lipstick, lip gloss - bright, then wipe it
away. I am big eyes bold yet, green too tired,
              giant smile and laughter.
                    Then hide it for a while.
I am blonde hair in a black mood.
Look at me,
         mirror mirror,
               no judgements.
                    Look at you.

SIXTEEN

It wasn't wrong, but it wasn't right.
We stayed on the border of safe, never completely crossing
lines, but knowing it could happen at any time.
Come closer. Stay back. We were ridiculously coy with our
teasing. Will life allow you one chance or does this change
lives for the worse?
Do we make life happen or does it happen to us?
Truth be told...all I wanted was your arms.
All you wanted was to hold me.
And so we did. In safe places. In public.
Never alone was our silent agreement.
Alone would mean wrong.
You held me for hours in that dim run down bar.
We looked like long time lovers.
We held hands like teenagers in a possibly random library.
We stayed warm in a blizzard inside your car.
I inhaled your boy scent like it was the last time I ever would.
Because it was.
We both knew if I looked up at your face we would've kissed,
ruining the innocence.
We would never know how to get back to just arms.
Goodbye was in an empty parking lot, saying words that lacked
depth.
We had replayed sixteen,
breaking our own hearts.
Again.

UNFORTUNATE

Break me and take me.
I gave it all so weakly,
oblivious to the way you kidnapped my thoughts.
It was an accidental misfortune of obvious proportions
                to my fantastical
                        romantical
                                brain.
We were victims and martyrs changing roles,
    bedroom games along with stomach pain.
  The wrong of us was a disease that infected,
and fuck, it was so powerfully connected.

REALIZATION

I can't be anyone's anything right now,
and this honesty to myself
is scaring me to death.

(If nothing else, we can be self aware.)

THERE WILL BE WOLVES

You will need to learn to save yourself.
There are wolves out there,
and they will eat you alive
like your flesh was made to be hunted.

DOMINANT

She is both a sinner and a saint.
Loving her means taking over when she hesitates.

HARDER

I can't be loved hard enough.
I'm greedy,
selfish,
almost crazy wanting more.
In my face compliments,
hands all around…
Let me act like it's too much,
when it's everything
and probably still not enough.
Want me in public.
Stay so fucking proud.
Love me more,
always more, completely
insanely
loud.

YES SIR

"I want you to be bad for me. Just me."

As if I'd have it any other way.

"You bring out this smirk and my bite.
Your growl catches my ear releasing
                        all inhibitions and fear."

I go down.
Yes Sir.
Yes Sir.
Yes Sir.

ULTIMATE PLAN

I've taken the road less traveled...
driven off the beaten path,
swerved in and out of traffic
and rediscovered my laugh.
Break rules with me.
Let's change lives and believe.
Just because I lived with destruction
doesn't mean I don't know happiness
is the ultimate plan.

RAW

He saw me broken, raw, and as real as I've ever shown another soul.
Wild eyed, hair a mess, something awoke in me.
I let my body tell him so.

INTIMATE

I have discovered that I've such a fondness for nicknames
and the intimacy they carry.
I have no willpower with neck kisses...none at all.
A tug of my hair, right underneath
when no one can see,
will always be my favorite game.
But, actually seeing more than lust in their eyes...
that's what pulls me in.

THAT KIND OF GIRL

She's the kind of girl you may not always know what to do with.
There is the teasing, sassy, I know I'm cute strut...
followed up with the
   tell me,
    tell me,
     tell me,
because she's drowning in fear
big-eyed look.
But that girl you can't understand...
that's the DREAM.
You make exceptions for her.
When she has that fear, you come back stronger,
take her by the shoulders and make her stay.

GOAL

I hope one day you wake up
with a smile in your stomach
and a hunger for life that you can't explain.

(We can't predict the future but we can choose to enjoy the
ride.)

SELF AWARE

I hope that you won't just dance.
But you'll be strong enough to expose your sadness
along with those sparkles,
and show them how you can still light up a room.

ROSE TINTED

I swear he sees me through rose tinted glasses.
It happens so many times I actually start to believe.
He is gentle hands holding my butterfly wings.
He is hair pulling at all the right times so I can't breathe.
And he stays.
He listens to me cry.
Hurting, not knowing what to say from his place,
outside my fear,
far far away.
But he stays.
I push.
He stays.
I pull.
He stays.
He teaches me unconditional.
He teaches me you don't need to hold on so tight…
because there is truth to love and loyalty.

SEXY

He calls me "Sexy" like it's my name.
An instant smile appears and I'm the most beautiful
woman in the room.
I'm craving his hands,
and loving too soon.

(There is the fear of getting burned, but I can not resist the
flame.)

TAKE THIS OFF

Wrapped up closer,
bodies needing to
take all this off.
I've got a feeling.
Undress faster.
Mind
   what
      manners?
Give all that's important
  and make you
  only for me.

(...and all of a sudden I am possessive.)

EYES AND CURVES

All of a sudden, through the magic of words, I feel like he's a wolf...
so damn hungry for my storyteller eyes and delicate curves.

LIKING

Find someone you like.
Like their smile and their eyes, those will never change, not
even as twenty years fly by. Find someone who enjoys things
that you do, make weekends full, separate and together.
Deep down know that you like life through similar eyes, spirits
finding friends for life. Make sure you see the sunrise and
sunset in the same beautiful colors. Are you both looking for
it...appreciating the sight? Most of all, treasure what makes
them smile. Unselfishly love what they're about.
If you don't want to be a part of what makes that smile grow,
your heart will never bring everlasting love to follow.
Sadly, you're better off alone.
Find someone you like,
and let them fall into like with you.

(In the right pair of hands I turn into magic. Abracadabra, Baby.)

FOREVER US

In a world so filled with hate, we will rise above...
stubbornly fighting
to continuously trust in love.
Living forever
on that line between
dirty and
sweet,
excitement shining from eyes
that still believe.

SAVORY

Filled with a crazy sense of delight..
I'm savoring the taste of
your name,
plus my name,
rolling off my tongue.

PARTS

You will always be my favorite part.
And the sum of your parts
added to the sum of my parts
will equal a total
of all that is... everything.

THUNDER

He felt like thunder,
like clouds rolling over the ocean
and the sweat underneath my long blonde hair.
He was like sand, clinging to me everywhere...
relentless in his pursuit to take over my skin.
And I wanted it.
I wanted his gentle kiss like sun
before the lightning of our hungry tongues.
Then the rain,
slick wet drops on street drums pounded
over and over in my head,
until the morning and he
had me making the softest sounds...
Rolling like thunder in our love soaked bed.

ALLOWED

Tell me all the places I'm allowed to exist.
I'll go there
    and pretend
        you're on your way
            home.

ANYTHING

Say something, like how much you might love me.
Say something, and we'll pretend like you never did.

(I heard the inflection in your voice...the rise in the weight of
the sigh as you let me down. I clearly heard you saying you
almost loved me.)

INEVITABLE

Especially in the dark like this, it's impossible to escape the
too good scent of her skin.
It's inevitable she'll pull you in.
The foolish side of you believes you have control,
    until she parts lipstick red lips and you actually hear
sunlight, and see two hearts letting go.

LETTERS

A six page love letter arrived in the mail today.
I knew one day it would come. I obviously knew what it
would say.
And I just want to say I'm sorry.
I just want to say I care.
I just want to say I don't understand it myself, but it was
real, I swear.
I shouldn't have made such promises. I shouldn't have let
you fall. There is nothing you did, nothing you said, so stop
beating your head against the wall.
A reason, a season, a lifetime.
You were a season, with a reason that I can't figure out. I
know you wanted to be my lifetime. And I know what it feels
like to be crushed.
And I know what it feels like to have your heart come out of
your mouth and there is no place to put it.
And I know that the ache feels like choking, drowning and
starving to death... like putting your hand straight into fire.
I know this, and yet I can't give you what you want.
Because if I told you I loved you, I'd only be feeding you a lie.
So, in response to that six page love letter...here is the ugly
truth... My last line needs to be goodbye.

BRAVERY

And even though I fear the fall, and the height, and the
possibility of the crash...
I will not let the same monster that broke me
lock me up for the rest of my life.

STRIDE

No need to tiptoe around the obvious
when all signs point me to you.
Walk hard and fast and claim me the way I want you to.

SAFE

I find myself on solid ground with you, and I'm
unfamiliar with how to stand.
Stumbling,
    falling,
       faltering a bit,
          yet still noticing the constant outstretch of your hand.

LINES

There is a fine line between love and hate.
We dance right there like we've lost all sense of
direction, forgetting how ghosts affect all the little ways we
change.

MAD LOVE

He realizes that sometimes I feel like the sky is falling.
So, we hold hands while he patiently watches it not collapse
on me. That's why I'll always have mad love for him.
Acceptance is kind of everything.

PEACE TALK

I think perhaps your skin speaks peaceful words to my lungs.
With a simple touch of your hand to my arm, my breath
becomes effortless once again.

DISCUSSIONS

Tell me what the stars say to you about me.
I'd be curious to know of the honesty in your discussions.

FIND THAT

Find someone who looks at you with adoration…
kisses you in the middle of a conversation
or in the middle of the night,
for no reason,
except because they need to.
Let them be someone that stands up for you in
every situation.
Find someone who pulls you in by the waist and whispers,
"you're so fucking beautiful,"
or "I'm so incredibly lucky,"
or "I need to take your clothes off right now."
Find someone who sees a teammate in you, as well as a
lover…
someone who wants to love you damn loud, and fucking
proud.
Make sure you absolutely look at them the same way.
Be amazing together.
Everywhere.
Find someone who makes you feel super sexy,
so in turn you can become your most uninhibited.
Find someone who loves your mind,
and your face, and craves your presence,
and needs your taste.
Yeah. Find that.

HE SAYS

And he says, "Baby"
And that I'm perfect
And "I'll always be right here."
And he calls me a brat when I'm acting sassy
and it's sexy
And here we go
back and forth
because we change our dirty and our sweet
like waves, it comes subtly-
then all at once
and I'm biting
and he's growling
and I soften from a look
and I need you
and then we're gentle,
settling into a peaceful everything
lost in eyes,
so many words spoken within a look.

SHOCKED

I'm captured in the truth behind those green lover boy eyes,
with my heart living shocked and happy,
yet in complete and utter surprise.

EXPOSED

I challenge you to love me harder than everything.
I dare you to let yourself be more.
My hands in the air, but it's your heart all exposed and
completely bare with absolutely nothing to break your fall,
except me.

ADMIT IT

I want you to admit it.
Lock eyes with me.
Lie down and wipe the tears and stop the shudder of sighs
that gasp from me...
and confess.
I am your weakness.
Tell me that the thought of another man's hands
makes you sick with jealousy.
And all you really want in this life
is you...
plus me.

HERE AND THERE

I fell in love with you in those moments between our kisses.
That sizzling hot but beautifully sweet minute before we let
go.
I fell in love with you there
and I stay in love with you here...(hand on heart.)

STRONG

Passion like ours will never fade
because we're not afraid to admit how much we feel for each
other. You taste like everything I've always wanted,
so I'm down on my knees giving you all of me,
in every way I can possibly love you.

(Let's show them that romance is alive and poetry isn't dead.)

ROAM HERE

He is hungry all day.
She is the wild place where he roams,
letting him give in to his most intense cravings.
A meal he is never finished with.
His mind falls to places darker here,
because he seems to need her more than the sun.
Patience, she whispers,
but he doesn't know of any such thing.
He demands,
and she feels it throughout her body…
a call to all the ways he wants her.
His hands finally upon her waist,
his eyes search for clues as to how she can feed
him in that moment.
With a nod, a small yes,
off with her dress and the rest.
They are a mess of desire, greed, lust, love and
sex.

(He made me feel so beautiful…
I just couldn't help the way my body danced in
response.)

PRAYING

I'm patiently craving
with eyes closed,
lips praying
that I'm the only one for you...
and you're falling into forever and always
with me.
Let the wild in my eyes
be the place you set yourself free.

THE ONES

The ones that notice (right upon meeting)
that the world sits on your shoulders (without permission)
and your heart is three times bigger than all the other girls'...
Those are the people you need to let stay (trust).

MORE

When everyone else said,
"You are just entirely too much,"
he reached out and said,
"Give me more of you to love."

WAVES

We swim the same wavelength, feeling each other out...
bravely charting beautiful new territory.
You are as wild as the river, yet as calm as a cove.
I dip my toes in, eager to know.

CHANCE

Because if you don't take the chance…
all we will ever be is a memory,
locked in a moment,
wrapped in a wish.

SOUL FOOD

I've never tasted anything this good for me.
You are truly food to my soul...
loving me like you've been starving.

(We didn't expect this journey, but my oh my does it seem like
the right way to go.)

I'M FLYING

Barefoot in the sand his eyes look to mine.
I'm a mess, ocean swept.
Our skin has been loved by the sun.
The air is hot and loud and the kids are finding seashells;
having fun.
And then he is on his knees...
not one knee but both,
face pressed into my sex.
I can't seem to look away from his mouth.
Yes, of course yes. Always for you yes.
Ridiculously in love with you yes.
Forehead kisses,
then tippy toe,
then salty tears slipping down my long sundress.
We will be officially bound
like the moon to the sky.
All my I love you's come out in a stream of nonsense,
while your words are somehow solid declarations growling in
my ear. I'm flying.
Yelling for the kids to come closer,
I kiss them all like crazy as you shake your head and joke.
Look, I show them and stick out my hand.
I'm smiling
I'm crying
I'm flying.
Then everyone is on us,
and we are a pile of love and celebration.
I think I am so full right now.
I'm in Heaven.
You take my hand in the midst of all the chaos and bring it
to your lips to kiss.
Holding it there, I watch your eyes close in thought.
These emotions are almost too much for my body to hold.
Bringing myself closer to you makes it easier to breathe.
Then you push aside my tangled hair, you bite my sweaty
neck and whisper..."I'm flying."

THIS WAY

She danced in his affection
letting it wash over her like rain,
kissing devotion into his soul…
Saying
"thank you for loving me
this way."

(You deserve a wild love from a gentle soul.)

LUCKY

All at once I'm lucky.
I'm blessed by the knowledge that you exist.
Wherever I am
it matters not
because I can feel you
filling the broken cracks of my heart.

YOU FIRST

I say
Baby,
tell me anything,
because my insides hurt.
I need a reminder that this is equal.
You whisper first.

EXPERIMENTS

Wearing smart girl glasses I will be spending my days doing
experiments. I need to find a solution on how to love you
harder. My theory is we will need a lot of kissing,
but it will all be for the sake of science.

FAVORITE EVERYTHING

You drape your arm over the back of her chair.
Gently sweeping the hair from her neck as you drink her in.
She's all yours, giving herself to you completely each day.
It's a blessing you recognize and it's breathtakingly erotic.
Rubbing your thumb over the base of her neck you, feel
compelled to devour her.
Waiting to have her seems impossible but you must,
yet the anticipation is a physical ache everywhere.
She arches slightly from the pressure of your thumb.
Her mouth opens a bit and she slowly turns to you.
Your favorite eyes.
She is literally your favorite everything.
That's the thing about her...she never hesitates to show
her love for you in return.
You can see it written all over her face
and your naughty thoughts seem to linger, jump in and mix.
Naughty or nice? Nice or naughty? It's all connected.
She stares, wide eyed, happy, and touches your scruffy
cheek. Leaning in closer, she whispers, "I love you," and
takes a playful bite of your bottom lip.
She pulls back and you lose her eyes,
so instead you trace the delicate lines of her collarbone,
forcing yourself not to kiss her.
She has been the only one since the moment you met.
Her words are real. Her heart is real.
She's your magic, and with her your soul shines brighter.
Gripping her upper thigh under the table,
you count the minutes until her eyes and mouth can return
to you...
until the actual moments you can spill into her,
becoming one.

RARE

I am drowning in the way that you look at me,
lost in the way that you care.
I have given up on all hope of recovery,
because this thing that we have found is so rare.

RANDOM SUNDAY

When he asked her, he had no ring.
It was an out of the blue pure emotion kind of thing.
They had woken up on a random Sunday morning in twisted
covers. They'd fucked all night.
And that morning with his eyes shining bright, she felt his
happiness like sunlight. He calls her 'Beautiful,' instead of
her name. He is the kind to mark his territory. Each time she
comes, he seems to be staking his claim. And yes, he has her.
She seems to amaze him. He brings the coffee exactly how she
likes it and climbs back into the soft messy blankets. The sun
peeks in through the blinds, making the dust in the air sparkle
like diamonds. Her hair is a crazy mess. He thinks she has never
looked so delicious. Setting their cups to the side, she rubs
her lips against his scruffy chin. There is nothing remarkable
about that morning, but he tells her he is so in love. Skin to
skin wrapped around, they watch each others faces. It's always
been in the eyes with them.
"Baby, I love you too." She can read his face like he can read
hers. She kisses his ear and holds his chest tighter.
"No Beautiful, I'm IN love with you." he becomes serious.
She stops, and propping up on her elbow, looks at him closer.
She kisses him slow and hard as if trying to bind them
somehow. Suddenly, he flips her over so he is looking down at
her face. He traces her lips with his thumb, and whispers what
she truly hadn't expected.
"Will you marry me?"
Silence. For some reason she is stunned.
Her mind races, thinking THIS is how a proposal is supposed to
feel...wow. Then, in a rush of what seems like five hundred
emotions, she gushes "yes" while tears are streaming down
onto the pillows. He wipes them and kisses salty lips, now
hungry with desire and possession. Her mind skips all over the
place and can't seem to settle down. She thinks..."He is so good
with me. I want to make him happy all the time. He's mine..."
and then he's inside her. She claws at his back unable to get
close enough. He's doing the same. They are trying to get under
each other's skin, the connection is that strong.

He goes down on her right away, and makes her come for the second time that morning.

Both of them, content and smiling, cuddle again. They hold hands. "Tomorrow, we'll get you a ring, baby."

"You already had me, you know that?" she smiles.

"Yes," he says, "but I want the whole world to know. This is it." Yes. This is it, and this is no longer like any other random Sunday.

THE LONG WAY

Let's take the long way home…
making sure to live the kind of life where we thrive on
nights out to keep our eyes lit up.
I'll want to survive on compliments I'll never ever get used to.

PEACE

Suddenly there is this new sort of peace surrounding me,
something I can't deny.
Thank you.
Thank you,
I whisper to your beautiful eyes.

IN DREAMS

In my dreams I get to be your girlfriend...and it's more than just a title you've smiled upon me. We've grown together like vines, and roots and have fallen... over and over...like leaves. The sunshine knows, and the moon oversees.
In my dreams, I am your home.
In your arms I'm locked. Your mouth is the one and only precious key. This is the body you gather your love to. I am where you feel peace, until my breath quickens and we become suddenly slick with desire and release.
I am your whisper.
I am your scream.
In my dreams, we have tomorrow.
We have friends that know us and laugh at your overly happy eyes, or at your hand constantly wanting mine (but I adore the safe space of you around me.)
In my dreams...we admit that it's fate.
My thank you's collapse onto yours as we show everyone how true love forever endures.

FOR KEEPS

We are dancing,
slow and sexy,
on that line
between sweet
and dirty and meaningful.
He stops my tears
and makes me laugh.
I want him to look at me for keeps,
and I think this music of ours
should never end.

WEEKENDS

We are sexy Saturday nights,
almost but not quite kissing...
leaning closer, just one barstool, inhibitions clearly missing.
Feeling like falling stars, not caring where we are,
making out with windows open,
lights bright, sounds ON.
We are Sunday mornings with coffee extra cream, messy
hair and lazy me.
Forcing errands until it's nap time.
Your hands warming my goose bumped skin...
sighing comfortably because this is true love we've crashed
upon,
and fallen in.

HERO

Some nights I just want a hero to tell me I'm too pretty to cry, while kissing my tears with his fingertips...tracing my flesh in lullabies.

SOULMATE TIME

It's in the eyes,
  in our hands.
  It's between our lips.
Down my throat,
      between my legs,
        lift my hips.
  It's your mouth.
It's in my heart,
  on your mind.
    No space empty
      lovingly fucking
       soulmate time.
You are the dirty, the sweet,
  absolutely my everything.

PREPARE

I will not fall easily.
It will be an ugly unexpected,
bursting into tears type of moment…
So lovers beware: I have the power to drown.
You might sink in the hurricane of my words.
Prepare your hearts now.

PREPARE

I will not fall easily.
It will be an ugly unexpected,
bursting into tears type of moment…
So lovers beware: I have the power to drown.
You might sink in the hurricane of my words.
Prepare your hearts now.

BEAUTY IN THE LET GO

I inked the forced independence upon my skin
letting them in without letting them in,
until time gave way to understanding;
the only path to heal is with learning to feel.
Loving yourself and forgiving all else...
Breathing with patience and
appreciating what you have with a heart that
overflows because there truly is beauty in the let go.

I'M SORRY

This need to apologize for being a burden never seems to escape me. The weight of myself, colored blue…
I will always say I'm sorry for crushing you.

(I'm working on this.)

SUMMERTIME STORMS

I dreamt of us making love during summertime
thunderstorms. The way your tongue would make my legs
shake turning each climax into an earthquake.
And us being us,
too wrapped up in our love,
would be unable to hear
all the passion pouring like rain.
The desperate declarations
and confessions of two hearts,
leaving us to appear as only crazy shadows
moving in the dark.

STARING CONTEST

We get caught up in the beauty we have found in each
other's faces. It's like we are teenagers again, instead of
having our second chance at romance. On the phone we
discuss our days and the laughter flows. We are like
teasing friends, but when our eyes meet, there is a silence
that stops us.
I'll watch you bite your lip. You'll watch me shaking my head
"Yes."
Yes to everything.
Yes to everything in the world as long as I'm holding hands
with you.
At times I'll challenge your eyes in a lover's staring contest.
At other times, I tuck my face and hide. You make me blush
with the way you adore me so openly. I love it. I want this
kind of life. These silences should not stop.
Our eyes are telling the stories of our hearts. And damn it,
our bodies want to participate. Of course, with just one kiss,
we both win this lover's staring contest.

THE SCENT OF HIM

He smelled like escape.
like wild,
like roaming,
like free...
I stood on tip toe and decided to live right there,
on his chest,
with hands that made a home all over me.

STEADY

How you stand there
so tall
so strong
with that umbrella
unwavering in my storm;
that right there is the reason I keep running to you.
You're the sunshine after my fall.

(He shows me over and over that, there, can be a high that
won't be followed by a crash,
and I'm flying.)

YOU WILL KNOW

You will know
because your smile will not just be on your face but in your
stomach...
deep down where those butterflies danced on your first
date. That smile will last over time pleasantly surprising you.
You will believe in him or her and love and things that can't
be seen. You may fight it because feeling good is something
we are taught to feel guilt for. But without a doubt nothing
will feel as powerful as falling into their arms.
You will know
when noticing each of your walls beginning to crumble.
You will know when you think of each other first,
when life isn't all about you and that protective instinct
kicks in. You will know when you realize you are on the same
team, not fighting each other -
this is your ride or die, and fuck, yes, you want to live forever
with that person by your side.
You will know
when you can make eye contact, in public, and even make
crazy declarations professing your luck,
and then the joking turns sweeter at times,
and perhaps becomes a kiss and a whisper.
You will know
when forehead kisses are thank you notes and you want to
give them all the time.

MATCH

His insides match his outside.
I'm stunned by the perfection of this
each time his heart calls out to mine.

(Life isn't as pretty as poetry, but you are beautiful like art.)

TO GET TO ME

There is so much want in his greed,
so much fire in his suffering.
This way that he reaches out,
desperately seeking
anywhere on my body,
a home for his mouth to land.

TASTE

I write like I believe in words that mix with imagination
might actually come true.
And I have such a taste for dreams,
I really do.

GLORY

Falling in love will never be planned.
It's irrational and maddening.
Yet, within the chaos lies a brilliant moment
where your heart feels like a sunrise
in all its beautiful glory.

TRIP

I look up and his green eyes
    spin
        me
           down.
Somehow he gets me drunk and high,
all at once…
a trip,
        I'll ride for life.

SECRET

I have a secret.
There is still time in this life to be surprised.
Hang on.

KEEP GOING

You've made it this far,
you might as well keep going with that never-settling type
attitude.

(Never settling looks good on you.)

HAPPY

I've decided it's okay to believe in what is happening between us. Happiness will no longer be a concept I fear.

I WILL HEAR YOU

I wanted to show you something to let you know I understand.
I'm not saying it to be sympathetic or because I feel required to.
I want to write these words because a part of me is just like a
part of you. And I know it's going to be horrible sometimes...
reallly completely awful, but please, I beg you to hang on.
I want to offer you a promise, a gift, a plan, my heart and
perhaps a challenge...find me.
When that fucking cloud is darkest and it just won't pass, the
trees are bare and your breath is coming too fast or not at all...
find me. And say 'help.' Or write it. Or blink five times if you
can't get the letters out.
I will know it's worse than ever before. I will know now you are
at the bottom of the ocean floor and have forgotten how to
swim and I will hear you.
Listen to me.
I will hear you.
No questions.
I will hear you.
Everyone needs somebody. I am here for you.
I understand and I promise you will never be alone. Let's sit
along the ocean floor and learn to float while holding hands.

SPARKLY DIAMOND SOUL

Look at you with that sparkly diamond soul.
I can't seem to pull my eyes away.
There is so much goodness wrapped around your core of
grief that I am awestruck as to how you haven't unravelled.
Your strength is finely woven in blue vulnerability, and I know
fear still glistens in those eyes,
but you are simply stunning.
All your flaws have turned you into a masterpiece,
something that could never be duplicated.
You, with your sparkly diamond soul...are one of a kind.

THE RIGHT DOSE

He calms... talking me off of the edges I walk in my mind.
"Thank you," I sigh, as I come...

down.

(You are a ridiculously amazing constant in this life of fear and landslides.)

REAL GIRL

I will make mistakes, and
I will mess up.
But my real is so much prettier than your fake.

DREAM GIRL

I look like an escape from reality.
I walk in and out of thoughts
    ...well mostly IN.
Stumbling onto good idea
after good idea.
I like the one where you accidentally fall in love with me.
Perhaps I am a come alive
    little fantasy,
making up for the broken.
Your past is the past.
Come on now,
    and slow dance into more with me.

I DESERVE THIS

I believe the idea is to love ourselves so fiercely that we
begin to show them,
THIS is how I deserved to be loved.
Mirror my passion.
Sink your teeth into the heart of me.

REALIZATION

All of a sudden I just realized…
I want to sit on your lap at every party,
hold your hand at every event,
dance with you at every wedding,
and kiss you goodnight for the rest of my nights.

REPEAT THIS

Just because you've been through a bad thing,
doesn't mean you are a bad thing.

(You are kind of wonderful.)

WHITE FLAG

I can't simply wave that white flag for peace.
No.
I think I will make a dress out of it,
throwing myself around in a passionate dance
Til I cry out in pain
while begging I'm sorry,
because one person can only take so much.

WITH EACH STEP...

I will become more,
and the more
will be wild
and the wild
will be amazing because
it will be exactly who I was
supposed to be
before.

TAKE CARE

...and if you need me kissing your forehead this time,
I will be there.

(When the winds are wild, fly closer to me.)

GET OUT

I can still feel the pain of you beneath my skin.
You are stuck in my bones.
And it's ridiculous really, because there were so many things
that I was not,
that you wished I were.
And so many things that I needed,
that you were unable to give.
So, why is your face stuck in the marrow of my mind?
Please get your face out of my hope.
No longer will I be filled with your sickness,
and I don't like the taste of your disapproval in my mouth.

SAY GOODBYE

Your heart will be heavy,
but you'll know that it's what's right.
Time and vibes assured you it's okay
to say goodbye.
You won't feel it then, but one day soon,
you'll see it was better for
me to be me,
and you to be you.
More than anything we needed to save ourselves
to make the universe fall into place
for everything else.

BEAUTIFUL EVER AFTER

Let us love harder during the most wild of storms, and when the wind settles we will undress the past, showing the world there can be beauty after destruction.

ACKNOWLEDGEMENTS

This book would not exist without my genuine love for love. I will just always be that kind of woman, and I'm damn proud of it.

Nor would it exist without all the positive feedback I get from readers of Dirty Sweet Poetry. It gives me so much joy knowing my words are not only relatable, but can bring happiness, hope and feelings of acceptance. This adventure continually supports a growing confidence, untangling a previous internal struggle residing inside my head. With each piece of writing I give more acknowledgement to the power of words. Creativity saves lives. I can see it so clearly now, and I'm twisting it all into art.

A big thank you to all of my coworkers for making me laugh, even on the hardest days. You lovely college peeps really do somehow make me feel younger than I am. (*insert hair toss and sassy smile.) Thank you Samantha Wutz and Tim Hoskinson for caring about me outside of work walls...and for seeing Birds of Prey, as it was clearly the worst movie of all time. Tim, holiday shifts are only good when it's us. Sam, you really are an exceptional friend (and nurse), going above and beyond during my migraine-ice-pack troll-hair close-to-death moments. The world needs more humans like you. Steven, thank you for feeding my children and embarrassing me. Bill, eyeroll. The entire nursery staff, bless you for listening to my fast talking. And for saving crafting for me, and mugs, and good creamer. (Absolutely essential to all of our daily functioning.)

Kathy Molitor, I love you for a million reasons, but thank you beyond words for bringing me back to Earth when I actually have broken. Loudly. And naked. Yeah, anxiety attacks are weird. Team Blonde. I just need you in my life, end of story.

Serious applause to my editor, friend, and an all around extremely generous man Bob Urman. I literally could not do this without you, and you know how much that is true. I think we are partners in crime now. Book three?

Thank you Eric, for our responsible continued co parenting. I wouldn't have a brain to write at all without our tag team efforts. (Also, I am the best ex wife ever.)

Tyler, I am so damn proud of you. Dad, Mom and sisters...I do truly miss you.

To my incredible children. Truthfully...you two are more than everything. I could never find the right words to express the intensity of my love.
(Same heart, my butterflies.)

Printed in Great Britain
by Amazon

47932291R00095